WELCOME TO A WONDERFUL WORLD OF STICKERS!

The **OCEAN** is one of nature's most varied habitats, home to amazing animals of all shapes and sizes. Use the stickers in this book to create your own **MARINE MENAGERIE** – from **SHELLFISH** scuttling on the shore and **ORCAS** wandering the waves to the mysterious creatures lurking in the sea's dark **DEPTHS**...

Simply match each numbered sticker at the back of the book to the same number in the sticker grid!

Learn fun facts about each of the creatures you create!

You can even customise the scenes with some of the extra stickers at the back.

Use the checklist at the back of the book to tick off the things you find next time you venture to the sea!

Eventually, you'll have whole oceans to explore!

sticker grid

sticker sheet

Note: The sticker sheets can be pulled out so that you don't have to keep flicking to the end. Stickers are slightly larger than the areas they cover so no awkward white bits show through.

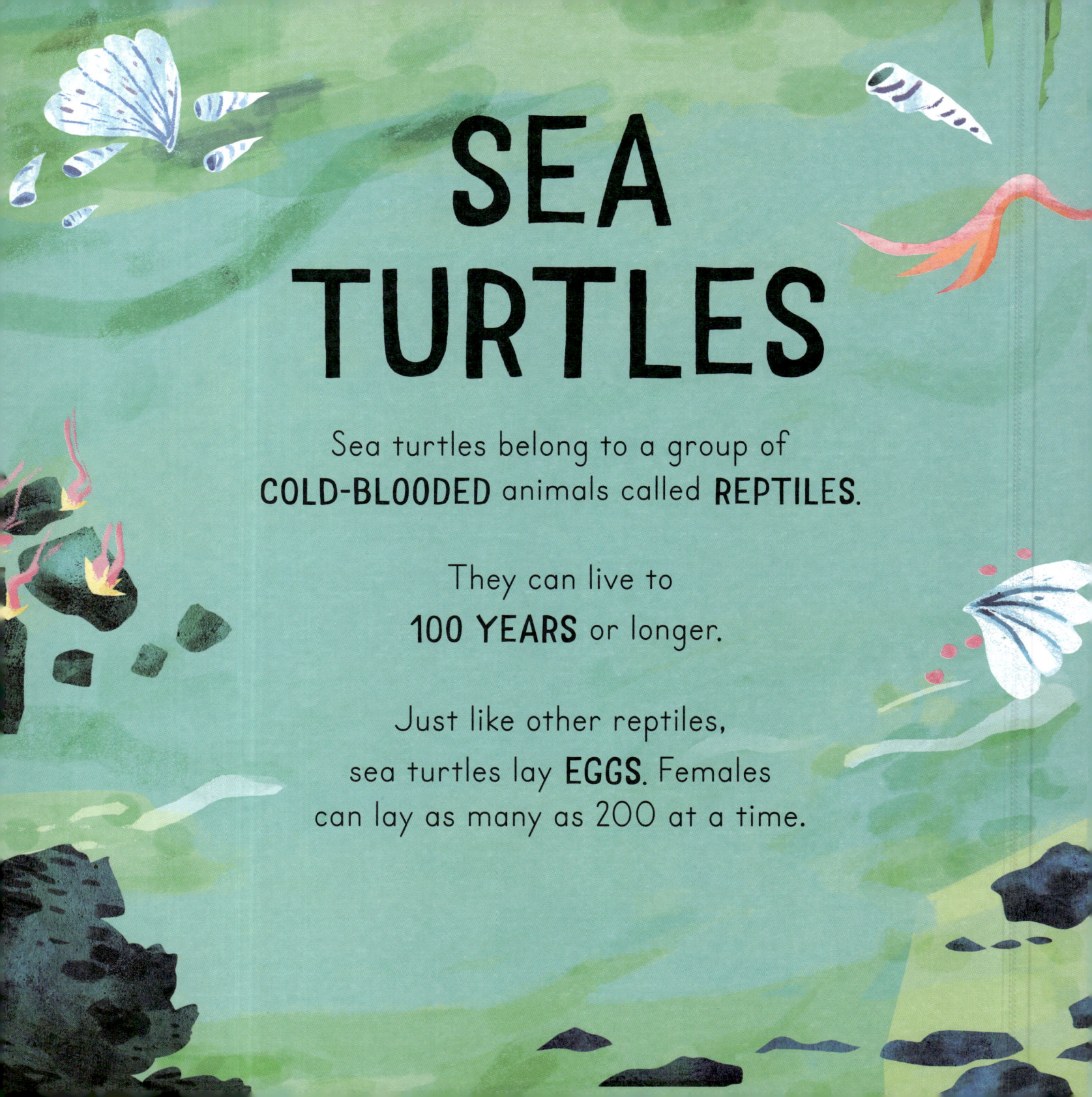

SEA TURTLES

Sea turtles belong to a group of
COLD-BLOODED animals called **REPTILES**.

They can live to
100 YEARS or longer.

Just like other reptiles,
sea turtles lay **EGGS**. Females
can lay as many as 200 at a time.

COLOUR WITH STICKERS

NATURE

OCEAN

FSC
www.fsc.org
MIX
Paper from
responsible sources
FSC® C135401

The Forest Stewardship Council® (FSC®) is an international, non-governmental organisation dedicated to promoting responsible management of the world's forests. FSC operates a system of forest certification and product labelling that allows consumers to identify wood and wood-based products from well-managed forests and other controlled sources.

For more information about the FSC, please visit their website at www.fsc.org

LITTLE TIGER

LONDON

CATERPILLAR BOOKS
An imprint of the Little Tiger Group
www.littletiger.co.uk
1 Coda Studios, 189 Munster Road, London SW6 6AW
Imported into the EEA by Penguin Random House Ireland,
Morrison Chambers, 32 Nassau Street, Dublin D02 YH68
Originally published in 2021
First published in Great Britain 2022
Text by Jonny Marx • Text copyright © Caterpillar Books Ltd 2021
Illustration copyright © Christiane Engel 2021
A CIP catalogue record for this book
is available from the British Library
All rights reserved • Printed in China
ISBN: 978-1-83891-343-4
CPB/2200/1995/1121
1 3 5 7 9 10 8 6 4 2

CLOWNFISH

Clownfish live near **ANEMONES**,
which are half-animal and half-plant!
Anemones have **TENTACLES** that **STING**,
but the clownfish aren't affected.

Anemones provide a safe
place for the clownfish to live.
If a **PREDATOR** comes close,
the anemones will sting it!

In return, the clownfish keep the anemones
clean by nibbling **ALGAE** and **DEBRIS**.

CRABS

The crab has its **SKELETON** on the outside of its body.

Some crabs are as small as a penny, while others have a leg span of up to 4m (13ft)!

Many crab species can **REGROW** limbs if they are damaged.

ORCAS

Orcas live in groups called **PODS**. Each pod is usually led by a mature female, who teaches the younger orcas to **HUNT**.

A large orca can grow to be 9m (30ft) in length — that's as long as a small truck!

Orcas are among the most **INTELLIGENT** animals on the planet.

SAILFISH

The sailfish is the **FASTEST** animal in the ocean.
It can swim at a speed of 110km per hour (68mph)!

The sailfish's **SWORD-LIKE BILL** is not
used for defence, but rather to
drive prey to shallower water.

Adult sailfish have few natural **PREDATORS**.
The other animals simply can't
catch this speedy fish!

SEAHORSES

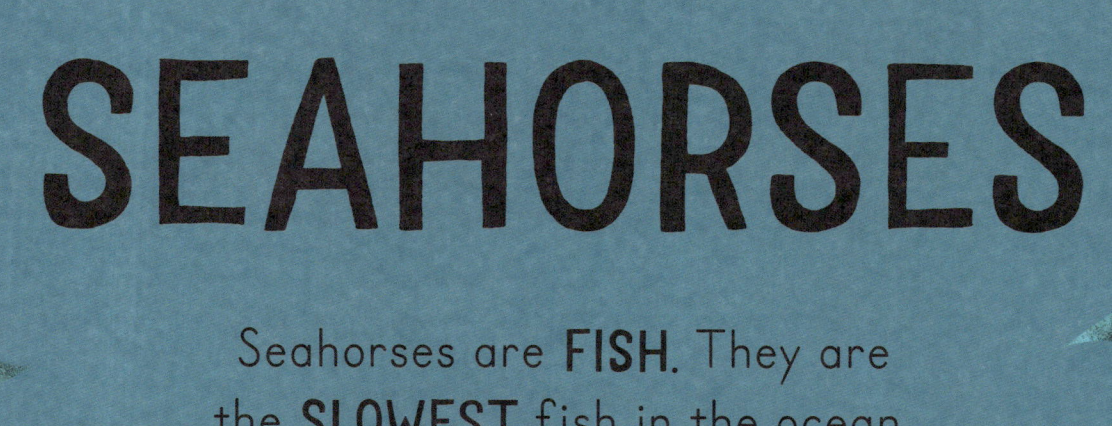

Seahorses are **FISH**. They are
the **SLOWEST** fish in the ocean.

A seahorse can **CLING** to plants and corals using
its tail. It can even cling to other seahorses!

Many species of seahorse use
CAMOUFLAGE to hide from predators.

ANGELFISH

Angelfish eat **SEA SPONGES** and **ALGAE**. They also nibble at the **PARASITES** living on other fish.

Saltwater angelfish live in **CORAL REEFS** in tropical waters. The reefs shield the angelfish from predators.

The angelfish has a **NARROW** body, which allows it to move and turn easily in tight spaces.

PENGUINS

The Galápagos penguin is the only penguin
species found in the northern hemisphere.
The rest live south of the **EQUATOR**.

Emperor penguins live in **ANTARCTICA**.
They can survive in frosty temperatures
as low as –50°C (–58°F) and in winds
of more than 200km per hour (125mph).

Penguins can drink **SEA WATER**.

STARFISH AND SEASHELLS

Most starfish have **FIVE** arms, but
some species have **10, 20,** or even **40**!

When it eats, a starfish pushes its
STOMACH out through its mouth and onto
its prey! Then the starfish pulls its stomach
– and its meal – back in through its mouth.

The **HERMIT CRAB** lives in a seashell.
When the shell no longer fits,
the crab finds a bigger one.

ANGLERFISH

Anglerfish live at the **BOTTOM** of
the ocean, where there is no light.

The female has an illuminated **LURE** on the top
of her head that she uses to attract prey.

Males are much smaller than females.
A male will attach himself to a female with
his teeth and absorb **NUTRIENTS** from her.

SPOTTER'S CHECKLIST

These are some things that you might see in and around the ocean. If you have a chance to visit the beach, check off all of the items that you see!

SEASHELL ◯

SEAGULL ◯

JELLYFISH ◯

CRAB ◯

STARFISH ◯

SEAWEED ◯

BARNACLE ◯

FISH ◯

DOLPHIN ◯

SEA TURTLES

CLOWNFISH

CRABS

ORCAS

SAILFISH

SEAHORSES

ANGELFISH

PENGUINS

STARFISH AND SEASHELLS

ANGLERFISH